THE OFFICIAL

RANGERS FOOTBALL CLUB

ANNUAL 2020

Written by Alan Clark
Designed by Mathew Whittles

A Grange Publication

© 2019. Published by Grange Communications Ltd., Edinburgh, under licence from Rangers Football Club. Printed in the EU.

Photographs © PA Images

ISBN 978-1-913034-28-3

CONTENTS

WELCOME
TO THE OFFICIAL RANGERS

I was delighted and hugely honoured to be confirmed as Rangers manager back in May 2018. That feeling remains as I look forward to what we can experience and achieve in the coming seasons.

When my staff and I accepted the roles at the club, we all said we were absolutely committed to bringing back success to you, the supporters, and this great club. Success at Rangers means silverware and although we didn't manage to win any trophies last season, I can feel happy with the progress we made from the beginning of the campaign to the end.

Continuing with our key players this season, complimented by the quality we've brought in that we hope will integrate quickly into the squad, we feel we are in a good position to build on the progress made last year. We know you, the fantastic supporters, will be with us every step of the way.

And that is why I know you will love picking up the Official Rangers Annual 2020, which once again comes packed full of stories, photographs, interviews, puzzles, quizzes – and much more. When I was a kid, I loved reading about all my favourite players and I know you will enjoy everything this annual has to offer.

ANNUAL 2020

❝ We feel we are in a good position to build on the progress made last year. **❞**

There is a section focusing on our first team squad, profiling each player, as well as a detailed review of the the 2018/19 season and our European run. You can read about a superb trophy-laden year all round for the academy teams, gain an insight into our Rangers Women's team and brush up on your knowledge of the club in the Historical A-Z feature.

Thanks again for your unwavering support and here's to a successful Rangers season.

Steven Gerrard

ALLAN McGREGOR

Position: Goalkeeper

Date of Birth: 31/01/1982

Place of Birth:
Edinburgh, Scotland

The veteran goalkeeper returned to Rangers last season as part of Steven Gerrard's first transfer window at the club and proved one of the best captures of last summer. Throughout the 2018/19 season, McGregor produced quality saves both at home in domestic competitions and across the continent in the Europa League. There is no doubt that the former Scotland No.1 will be an instrumental part of the team this season as well.

FACT:

McGregor has won 11 major trophies as a Rangers player, including three league titles.

WES FODERINGHAM

Position: Goalkeeper

Date of Birth: 14/01/1991

Place of Birth:
Hammersmith, England

The Englishman arrived from Swindon in Mark Warburton's first season and is now in his fifth year at Ibrox. A formidable shot-stopper, Foderingham was No.1 for three seasons and will hope for more time between the sticks this time around.

FACT:

Foderingham is one of the longest serving players in the current squad, having signed in 2015.

ANDY FIRTH

Position: Goalkeeper

Date of Birth: 26/09/1992

Place of Birth: Ripon, England

Former Liverpool goalkeeper Firth was signed from Barrow Town in January 2019 and the 23-year-old provides competition for McGregor and Foderingham. He made a brief appearance away to Kilmarnock in the last game of last season, replacing Foderingham for the last eight minutes.

FACT:

Firth came through the Liverpool youth ranks and left having spent 11 years in total at the club.

JAMES TAVERNIER

Position: Defender

Date of Birth: 31/10/1991

Place of Birth: Bradford, England

The right-back is in his fifth season at Rangers and over that period has developed and grown to be an essential part of everything the team is about. Gerrard named him captain at the start of 2018/19 and he took that honour in his stride, continuing to be a fantastic asset defensively and in attack. The skipper loves a penalty and in total he provided 17 goals and 20 assists last term.

FACT:

Skipper Tavernier broke John Greig and Sandy Jardine's goals record for a defender last season, scoring 17 in total.

MATT POLSTER

Position: Defender

Date of Birth: 08/06/1993

Place of Birth: Milwaukee, Wisconsin, United States

The American defender/midfielder signed for Rangers at the start of 2019 and played a limited number of minutes in the 2018/19 season, but he will be hoping to make his mark in this campaign. The ex-Chicago Fire player caught Gerrard's eye and Polster will have to be ready to step in at right-back or midfield when needed in what will prove to be a long season.

FACT:

Polster is one of a small group of Americans to have played for the Gers, with Claudio Reyna, DaMarcus Beasley and Carlos Bocanegra among the others.

CONNOR GOLDSON

Position: Defender

Date of Birth: 18/12/1992

Place of Birth: Wolverhampton, England

The former Brighton centre-half enjoyed a successful debut season at Ibrox and is now firmly first choice at Rangers. A big commanding defender, Goldson is useful at both ends of the park, proving to be a reliable part of the defence as well as providing a goal threat from set-pieces.

FACT:

The defender once scored seven goals in one season, playing for Shrewsbury Town in England's League Two back in 2014/15.

FILIP HELANDER

Position: Defender

Date of Birth: 22/04/1993

Place of Birth: Malmö, Sweden

The Sweden internationalist was a big summer signing for Rangers as the gigantic central defender signed from Italian side Bologna back in July. With over 80 games played in Serie A, as well as two league title wins for Malmö and several international caps, left-footed Helander provides top level experience for the Gers backline.

FACT:

The 6ft 4" stopper was named in Sweden's World Cup 2018 squad.

GEORGE EDMUNDSON

Position: Defender

Date of Birth: 31/08/1997

Place of Birth: Wythenshawe, England

A summer addition at the club from Oldham, Edmundson is a towering centre back with potential in spades. He has plenty of competition for a slot in central defence but at 21, the Englishman will be given time to bed in at Ibrox in his new surroundings.

FACT:

The Englishman only made his senior debut four years ago, playing for old club Oldham Athletic in the 2015/16 season.

NIKOLA KATIĆ

Position: Defender

Date of Birth: 10/10/1996

Place of Birth: Ljubuški, Bosnia and Herzegovina

Like Goldson, Croatian stopper Katić had been at the club a full season before the current campaign and has fully settled into his new life in Glasgow. Signed from Slaven Belupo last summer, Katić made 30 appearances and showed what his game is all about – a tall centre back with plenty of strength to defend at one end and provide a goal threat at the other.

FACT:

Despite being born in Bosnia, Katić holds Croatian citizenship and has played several times with the Croatia Under-21 side and has one cap with Croatia's top side.

JON FLANAGAN

Position: Defender

Date of Birth: 01/01/1993

Place of Birth: Liverpool, England

Signed from Gerrard's former club Liverpool when he himself joined the club last summer, the manager recruited Flanagan for use in both full-back positions. The Scouse defender filled in mostly on the left side as a squad option. His tenacity always proves useful to have in the team.

FACT:

The full-back made 51 appearances for Liverpool, including 25 in the one season at the English Premier League outfit.

BORNA BARIŠIĆ

Position: Defender

Date of Birth: 10/11/1992

Place of Birth: Osijek, Croatia

Croatia internationalist Barišić scored for Osijek against Rangers in the Europa League qualifiers last season and shortly after signed for Gerrard's charges. A mixed debut season, affected by injuries, was frustrating for the left-back but after a positive pre-season, Barišić is confident of proving his worth in this campaign.

FACT:

The left-back was one of two players signed from NK Osijek in Gerrard's first campaign, with Eros Grezda following shortly after.

ANDY HALLIDAY

Position: Defender

Date of Birth: 11/10/1991

Place of Birth: Glasgow, Scotland

Rangers through and through, the versatile Halliday is capable of filling in at a number of positions in the team, mainly left-back or central midfield. Under Gerrard last season, Halliday enjoyed a comeback at Ibrox by featuring in 35 games across the campaign. His versatility and passion for the shirt on and off the pitch will be needed again in another busy season.

FACT:

Halliday was brought up on Copland Road, the street parallel to the Copland Road Stand at Ibrox, known traditionally as the 'Rangers end'.

STEVEN DAVIS

Position: Midfielder

Date of Birth: 01/01/1985

Place of Birth: Ballymena, Northern Ireland

The Northern Irishman returned to the club he won several trophies with around a decade ago by arriving on loan from Southampton in January, but he made the switch permanent in the summer after a successful return. Davis' cool head and class on the ball helps Rangers' midfield to function smoothly.

FACT:

In both of the midfielder's spells at Ibrox, Davis was initially signed on loan for six months before penning a permanent deal.

GLEN KAMARA

Position: Midfielder

Date of Birth: 28/10/1995

Place of Birth: Tampere, Finland

The all-action Finnish midfielder has been in fantastic form since he swapped dark blue for light blue in January 2019. Kamara slotted right into the midfield, showing his passing skills and ball control to be exemplary. He'll continue to be a key part of Gerrard's midfield.

FACT:

Kamara came through the Arsenal academy having joined the club in 2012 and staying until 2017.

JOE ARIBO

Position: Midfielder

Date of Birth: 21/07/1996

Place of Birth: London, England

Another of the summer additions, Aribo left Charlton Athletic after helping them achieve promotion to the English Championship and is a goalscoring, box-to-box midfielder. Signed in the summer 2019 transfer window, Aribo could prove to be a superb bargain for Rangers if he fulfills his potential at Ibrox.

FACT:

Aribo played in the English League 1 play-off final as Charlton Athletic defeated Sunderland at Wembley, almost exactly a month before arriving at Rangers.

SCOTT ARFIELD

Position: Midfielder

Date of Birth: 01/11/1988

Place of Birth: Dechmont, Scotland

Another all-rounder in the midfield engine room is Arfield, who was one of Rangers' best players in the last campaign. Capable of playing in different midfield roles as well as linked up with a striker in an inside forward position, Arfield scored a memorable Old Firm goal against Celtic back in May and Gerrard will depend on his quality again.

FACT:

Despite being born in Scotland and playing for different Scottish age groups, Arfield plays his international football for Canada, qualifying through his Toronto-born father.

RYAN JACK

Position: Midfielder

Date of Birth: 27/02/1992

Place of Birth: Aberdeen, Scotland

The central midfielder has been a mainstay for Rangers ever since he made the switch from Aberdeen back in the summer of 2017. Jack is calm on the ball, can read opposition attacks very well and generally provides stability as a deep-lying player. An Old Firm-winning goal last December is still fresh in the memory for the Gers fans.

FACT:

Midfielder Jack made exactly 250 appearances for Aberdeen over seven seasons before his move to Rangers in 2017.

GREG DOCHERTY

Position: Midfielder

Date of Birth: 10/09/1996

Place of Birth: Milngavie, Scotland

Fresh from a season-long loan spell down at Shrewsbury Town, Docherty is back in Rangers blue and contributing to the team's successes in his natural central midfield position. After scoring and assisting plenty while down in League 1, Gerrard brought him back into the fold for this season and the boyhood Gers fan is working hard to claim a regular spot.

FACT:

Docherty scored the only goal for Hamilton in the two-legged 2016/17 Premiership play-off against Dundee United, ensuring Accies' safety.

ANDY KING

Position: Midfielder

Date of Birth: 29/10/1988

Place of Birth: Barnstaple, England

Arriving in mid-August on loan from Leicester, Welsh internationalist King adds to the quality in the central area for Gerrard to pick this season. Throughout his career he has shown consistent displays, as well as chipping in goals, and is Leicester's highest scoring midfielder ever. He's had loan spells at Swansea City and Derby County on top of ten seasons at the Foxes, including making 29 appearances in 2015/16 when they won the Premier League title.

FACT:

With Leicester City, he won the English League One title, Championship title and Premier League title in 2009, 2014 and 2016 respectively – the first and only player to win the top three divisions with the same team in the Premier League era.

SHEYI OJO

Position: Forward

Date of Birth: 19/06/1997

Place of Birth: Hemel Hempstead, England

Highly rated by European champions Liverpool, Ojo signed a season-long loan deal in the summer to play for Rangers and develop his game. The young winger has made a great impression in his Gers spell so far and the talented Englishman will be hoping an increase in game time from previous loans will bring out the best of him.

FACT:

Rangers is the fifth team that Ojo has been loaned to by parent club Liverpool, the others being Wigan Athletic, Wolves, Fulham and Stade Reims.

GREG STEWART

Position: Forward

Date of Birth: 17/03/1990

Place of Birth: Stirling, Scotland

Signed from Birmingham City on a free transfer in the summer, Stirling-born Stewart will provide competition for places in a few attacking positions this season. Gerrard will be hoping he can rely on Stewart, who had loan spells at Aberdeen and Kilmarnock last season, to help break down stubborn defences and bring something different to his final third ammunition.

FACT:

Stewart was at Rangers before this spell but in a very different capacity, having spent some time in the academy teams before being released at the age of 13.

JAMIE MURPHY

Position: Forward

Date of Birth: 28/08/1989

Place of Birth: Glasgow, Scotland

The former Motherwell and Brighton winger will want a fair crack of the whip this season at Ibrox after missing out on the entire season last time through a horrific injury sustained in August 2018. He impressed with his guile and directness on the wing during the initial six-month loan spell he had from January to May in the 2017/18 season.

FACT:

Murphy has 205 appearances to his name in English football, having played for Sheffield United and Brighton in between his time at Motherwell and current club Rangers.

JORDAN JONES

Position: Forward

Date of Birth: 24/10/1994

Place of Birth: Redcar, England

After impressing in the Scottish game for Kilmarnock, Rangers stepped in to secure Jones on a pre-contract last season, allowing him to join up with the squad at Ibrox for the start of this season. A Northern Ireland internationalist, Jones will hope to hold down a regular place on the left wing with plenty of competition around at the club for a wide position this campaign.

FACT:

Winger Jones played 97 times for Kilmarnock in the Scottish top-flight before his Ibrox switch, scoring 11 goals for the Rugby Park side.

BRANDON BARKER

Position: Forward

Date of Birth: 04/10/1996

Place of Birth: Manchester, England

Signed in early August, Barker signed a three-year deal with the Gers from Manchester City having spent time on loan at Rotherham United, NAC Breda, Hibernian and most recently Preston North End. A well-known player to Ibrox director of football Mark Allen, who was a key figure at City's youth academy, Gerrard will be hoping the explosive English winger can develop his game and provide stiff competition to the likes of Jones in the wide left area of the team.

FACT:

Barker spent 15 years at Manchester City before making the move to Rangers, joining in 2004 at the age of eight and progressing through the academy system.

RYAN KENT

Position: Forward

Date of Birth: 11/11/1996

Place of Birth: Oldham, England

The transfer story that ran all summer long, the talented Englishman signed a four-year deal at the club on the last day of the transfer window. After an impressive loan spell from Liverpool last season, including a great solo goal away to Celtic, Steven Gerrard was keen to bring the winger back to Ibrox and eventually got his man. Wearing the number 14 jersey, Kent will play a key part in any success Rangers achieve this season with his skill, direct play and blistering pace.

FACT:

Kent has enjoyed his fair share of awards in his career having been named Barnsley's young player of the year in 2016/17. He also won Rangers' and PFA Scotland's equivalent accolades in 2018/19.

ALFREDO MORELOS

Position: Forward

Date of Birth: 21/06/1996

Place of Birth: Cereté, Colombia

The Colombian striker arrived at Ibrox for just £1million from Helsinki in 2017 and has proven time and time again to be integral to the Gers frontline, becoming a fan favourite at Ibrox. With 30 goals last season across the Premiership, Scottish Cup, League Cup and Europa League, Morelos was a striking sensation in blue and, now into his third campaign in Scotland, will no doubt prove to be a thorn in many a defender's side again this campaign.

FACT:

'El Bufalo' has finished the club's top goalscorer in the first two seasons since arriving from Finland, tying with Josh Windass on 18 and then notching 30 last term.

JERMAIN DEFOE

Position: Forward

Date of Birth: 07/10/1982

Place of Birth: London, England

The experienced former England striker became a Rangers player on an 18-month loan deal from Bournemouth back in January 2019 and was expected to add another dimension to the Rangers forward line. He did just that in the appearances he made in the second half of last season, either from the bench or from the start with Morelos unavailable, and if he can repeat that form – which saw him notch eight goals – then he'll be key for the Gers once more.

FACT:

Since 2004, Defoe has run out for the England national team on 57 occasions with a goal return of 20.

2018/19
SEASON REVIEW

Sunday 12th August 2018

Scottish Premiership
Rangers 2-0 St Mirren
Goals: Morelos, Goldson

Rangers marked the first home league game of the season with a win as the visitors from Paisley succumbed to a 2-0 defeat.

Alfredo Morelos got Steven Gerrard's men off to a great start as he first robbed Jack Baird of possession before running onto Jamie Murphy's through ball. The Colombian dragged his shot past the goalkeeper to open the scoring.

It was then 2-0 after just 24 minutes when new signing Borna Barišić whipped in a superb cross from a free kick on the right side, fellow new boy Connor Goldson meeting it with a great header.

Ross McCrorie was shown a straight red card just a few minutes later and despite playing an hour with ten men, the Light Blues saw out the game comfortably to claim three points.

RANGERS: McGregor, Flanagan, Goldson, Katić, Barišić (Tavernier 62), McCrorie, Kent (Halliday 69), Coulibaly, Ejaria, Murphy, Morelos (Sadiq 77).
Subs not used: Foderingham, Hodson, Candeias, Middleton.

Sunday 19th August 2018

League Cup Second Round
Kilmarnock 1-3 Rangers
Goals: Morelos (3)

It was the perfect day for talisman Alfredo Morelos at Rugby Park as the Gers got their League Cup campaign off to a flyer with this win in Ayrshire.

The Colombian grabbed a hat-trick to send Killie spinning out of the competition at the second round stage. His first goal came through the assistance of James Tavernier's cross with Morelos nodding it home, before the striker added a second when he turned a defender before rolling the ball across goal and into the net.

Borna Barišić's own goal gave the home side some hope but Rangers sealed the win late on in the second half when Morelos completed his treble of goals, tapping the ball in to finish off a well-worked move involving Scott Arfield and captain Tavernier.

The only blemish on the day was the injury sustained to Jamie Murphy which resulted in the winger being missing for the rest of the season.

RANGERS: Foderingham, Tavernier, Goldson, Katić, Barišić, Ejaria, Arfield (McCrorie 79), Halliday, Kent, Morelos (Sadiq 79), Murphy (Candeias 17).
Subs not used: Alnwick, Jack, Middleton, Flanagan.

Sunday 23rd September 2018

Scottish Premiership
Rangers 5-1 St Johnstone
Goals: Tavernier, Morelos, Arfield, Lafferty, Candeias

Ibrox was treated to a feast of goals on this sunny September afternoon as the Rangers comfortably saw off the challenge of the visitors from Perth.

Fresh from an impressive 2-2 draw away to Villarreal in the Europa League, the Gers continued good form in this league encounter with James Tavernier opening the deadlock with a perfectly hit free-kick.

Alfredo Morelos rifled in a left-footed effort after beating a defender inside the area before Scott Arfield made it three early in the second half, tapping in the rebound from a Ryan Kent blast that had smacked the crossbar.

Substitute Kyle Lafferty was the fourth Gers scorer as he calmly slotted the ball home before St Johnstone tucked away a penalty. Daniel Candeias got himself on the scoresheet to restore the four-goal lead as the Gers continued to hunt down early league leaders Hearts.

RANGERS: McGregor, Tavernier (Ejaria 56), Goldson, Katić, Flanagan, McCrorie, Candeias, Coulibaly (Dorrans 63), Arfield, Kent (Lafferty 71), Morelos.
Subs not used: Foderingham, Worrall, Halliday, Middleton.

Wednesday 26th September 2018

League Cup Quarter Final
Rangers 4-0 Ayr United
Goals: Katić, Middleton (2), Morelos

Steven Gerrard fielded a slightly different starting XI for this League Cup clash and it paid dividends with a thumping 4-0 victory.

Croatian defender Nikola Katić headed his side in front before youngster Glenn Middleton scored only his second senior goal for the Ibrox men shortly after.

Alfredo Morelos finished from close range early in the second half before Middleton grabbed his brace in the 70th minute to cap off a Man of the Match display against the Scottish Championship opposition, setting up a League Cup semi-final date at Hampden with Aberdeen.

RANGERS: Foderingham, Flanagan, Katić, Worrall, Halliday, Ross McCrorie (Kelly 69), Kent, Ejaria, Dorrans (Rossiter 56), Middleton, Morelos (Grezda 50).
Subs not used: Robby McCrorie, Goldson, Wallace, Arfield.

Sunday 7th October 2018

Scottish Premiership
Rangers 3-1 Hearts
Goals: Kent, Morelos, Arfield

Undefeated in the league and riding the crest of a wave at the top of the Scottish Premiership, Hearts arrived in Glasgow for this one full of confidence.

The form book was thrown out the window though as Rangers defeated the Jambos in ruthless fashion at Ibrox with a comfortable victory. Ryan Kent beat a peculiar offside trap to roll in the opening goal, before Alfredo Morelos back-heeled the ball high into the net with an outrageous goal.

Scott Arfield made sure of the win after just 32 minutes of the first half with the third goal, finishing off a move that saw a James Tavernier cross for Morelos saved by the goalkeeper.

Hearts had Michael Smith sent off and managed a consolation goal in the second half, but it had little bearing on the outcome.

RANGERS: McGregor, Tavernier, Goldson, Worrall, Flanagan, Coulibaly, Candeias (Lafferty 87), Arfield (Halliday 84), Ejaria (Jack 66), Kent, Morelos.
Subs not used: Foderingham, McCrorie, Katić, Middleton.

Sunday 21st October 2018

Scottish Premiership
Hamilton 1-4 Rangers
Goals: Kent, Tavernier (2), Morelos

Rangers ended up with three points and what looked like an emphatic win looking at the scoreline, but it was far from comfortable against the Accies that afternoon.

Ryan Kent raced onto the ball and finished with gusto near the internal to open the scoring for the Gers, before a sluggish second half saw little action until the home side equalised through Boyd on 80 minutes.

With time running out, the Gers needed a goal from somewhere and their urgent pressing was rewarded as the referee gave two penalties, both of which were converted by skipper James Tavernier, before a clever finish from Alfredo Morelos put a shine on the full time result.

RANGERS: McGregor, Tavernier, Goldson, Katić, (Worrall 79), Halliday, Coulibaly, Rossiter (Grezda 82), Ejaria, Candeias, Morelos, Kent (McCrorie 87).
Subs not used: Foderingham, Flanagan, Middleton, Sadiq.

Saturday 3rd November 2018

Scottish Premiership
St Mirren 0-2 Rangers
Goals: Candeias, Morelos

Another league game on the road and another challenge for the Light Blues that displayed their drive this season.

A slightly slower match between the sides in Paisley brightened up towards the end of the game with a spate of incidents as the Gers won 2-0.

Firstly, Daniel Candeias' cross from the right ended up landing in the back of the net to give his side a much needed opening goal in proceedings.

With time running out for St Mirren, Alfredo Morelos finished from a tight angle, as he so often does, to seal the three points before Candeias was controversially red carded.

RANGERS: McGregor, Tavernier, Goldson, Worrall, Halliday, Ejaria (Rossiter 87), Jack, Arfield, Kent, Morelos, Grezda (Candeias 55).
Subs not used: Foderingham, Flanagan, Katić, Coulibaly, Middleton.

Sunday 11th November 2018

Scottish Premiership
Rangers 7-1 Motherwell
Goals: Arfield (2), Tavernier, Morelos, Middleton, Grezda (2)

Rangers' impressive form at Ibrox in the first half of 2018 continued as they put seven past ten-men Motherwell in an all-conquering display.

Scott Arfield was at his attacking midfield best in the game and scored the first of a double after eight minutes, before James Tavernier scored from the spot and Alfredo Morelos headed in from a corner.

Motherwell had grabbed an equaliser just before Tavernier's penalty but Carl McHugh was given a second yellow for the penalty award, so it was already an uphill struggle for the Steelmen.

Glenn Middleton proved his worth after starting the game as he made it 4-1 with his drive, with Ryan Jack assisting Arfield for his double just two minutes later.

Substitute and new signing Eros Grezda then extended the scoreline in his side's favour with his first goals in the blue of Rangers to round off a great day's work for Steven Gerrard's outfit.

RANGERS: McGregor, Tavernier, Katić (McAuley 45), Worrall, Halliday, Jack, Grezda, Arfield, Ejaria, Middleton (Atakayi 73), Morelos (Lafferty 52).
Subs not used: Foderingham, Flanagan, McCrorie, Rossiter.

Saturday 24th November 2018

Scottish Premiership
Rangers 3-0 Livingston
Goals: Candeias, Morelos, Arfield

Having lost to the Scottish Premiership new boys on their patch in September, Rangers knew of the threat posed by Livingston and were ready to turn in a professional performance to clinch all three points at Ibrox.

Daniel Candeias got the ball rolling after 20 minutes, heading in a fantastic corner delivered by winger Glenn Middleton.

The Gers searched for a second goal to make things more comfortable and it started to look promising when Alfredo Morelos was brought off the bench after 62 minutes, the Colombian running Livi ragged before scoring a great goal on 83 minutes.

There was time at the end for Scott Arfield to get in amongst the goals again as he fired in a Morelos cross at the near post.

RANGERS: McGregor, Tavernier, Goldson, McAuley, Halliday (Flanagan 77), Jack, Candeias, Ejaria (Coulibaly 80), Arfield, Middleton, Lafferty (Morelos 62).
Subs not used: Foderingham, Worrall, Rossiter, Grezda.

Sunday 2nd December 2018

Scottish Premiership
Hearts 1-2 Rangers
Goals: Goldson, Morelos

Rangers went to the top of the league for the first time under Liverpool legend Steven Gerrard's managerial tenure as they made it four league wins on the spin.

With Celtic having played a game less, the Gers visited the capital knowing a win would put them ahead by a point and deliver a significant boost to the squad and fans alike.

Gareth McAuley was unfortunate as a cross deflected off the Northern Irishman and into the net for a Hearts opener, but the Light Blues fought back magnificently.

Connor Goldson bundled the ball in at the back post from a corner to level the match just a few minutes later, before James Tavernier's free-kick delivery was met on the volley immaculately by (who other than) Alfredo Morelos for 2-1.

Scott Arfield was given a straight red card in the second half but the Gers managed the game very well to see the victory out and celebrate becoming leaders.

RANGERS: McGregor, Tavernier, Goldson, McAuley, Halliday, Ejaria, Coulibaly (McCrorie 81), Arfield, Candeias (Lafferty 86), Morelos, Grezda (Jack 64).
Subs not used: Foderingham, Flanagan, Worrall, Middleton.

Sunday 23rd December 2018

Scottish Premiership
St Johnstone 1-2 Rangers
Goals: Morelos (2)

Following a few disappointing results in the month of December, this trip to McDiarmid Park was crucial for Rangers if they wanted to keep the pace in the title race.

And they left it late, having gone a goal down in the first half to a goal from St Johnstone's Matty Kennedy.

Steven Gerrard looked for some inspiration from his bench with Glenn Middleton and Kyle Lafferty making their way on, and it was the former who helped them get back on level terms with his superb cross from the left being met with a downward Alfredo Morelos header.

Lafferty's influence in a more direct style helped the Gers hugely in the second half and it was his knock down to James Tavernier that gave the Englishman the opportunity to cross for Morelos, who flicked the delivery into the net with tremendous skill for an 88th minute winner.

RANGERS: McGregor, Tavernier, Worrall, Goldson, Barišić, (Wallace 41), McCrorie, Halliday, Candeias, Coulibaly (Lafferty 56), Grezda (Middleton 45), Morelos.
Subs not used: Foderingham, Flanagan, Katić, Rossiter.

Saturday 29th December 2018

Scottish Premiership
Rangers 1-0 Celtic
Goals: Jack

Rangers defeated their arch rivals Celtic to end the calendar year level on points at the top of the Scottish Premiership table.

The scoreline didn't reflect the balance of play on the day as the Gers ran all over their Old Firm foes, creating many opportunities over the 90 minutes and testing Craig Gordon several times.

The winning goal came at 30 minutes, as superb wing play from Ryan Kent saw him leave Mikael Lustig stranded on the ground before he picked out Ryan Jack with a low ball. The midfielder side-footed the ball home via a slight knick off Scott Brown to send Ibrox wild.

The Ibrox men could and should have added to their one-goal advantage, but in the end the result was never in doubt as the Gers celebrated a memorable derby victory to see out the year on a massive high.

RANGERS: McGregor, Tavernier, Goldson, Worrall, Halliday, McCrorie, Jack, Arfield (Flanagan 92), Candeias (Coulibaly 71), Kent, Morelos.
Subs not used: Foderingham, Katić, Wallace, Middleton, Lafferty.

Sunday 27th January 2019

Scottish Premiership
Livingston 0-3 Rangers
Goals: Jack, Kent, Morelos

After the winter break and the disappointment of a 2-1 reverse at Kilmarnock the week before, Rangers travelled to the Tony Macaroni Arena determined to make amends.

It ended up being one of their most impressive away performances as they ran out 3-0 winners, Ryan Jack adding to his Old Firm goal with a long-range effort that Livingston goalkeeper Liam Kelly spilled into his own net.

Ryan Kent blasted in a second following a block by the Livi defence inside the 18-yard box as the Gers looked to add more goals to their display in West Lothian.

Alfredo Morelos wrapped it all up in style as he rounded Kelly to finish from an acute angle and send the Gers supporters home delighted.

RANGERS: McGregor, Tavernier, Worrall, Katić, Barišić (Halliday 82), McCrorie, Jack, Arfield, Candeias, Morelos (Defoe 76), Kent (Davis 76).
Subs not used: Foderingham, McAuley, Coulibaly, Middleton.

Saturday 2nd February 2019

Scottish Premiership
Rangers 4-0 St Mirren
Goals: Tavernier (2), Defoe, Kent

It was a game of penalties in this one as Rangers dispatched three out of the four that were awarded on the day at Ibrox.

James Tavernier could have had a hat-trick had he scored all three that he stepped up to take, the captain scoring two in the third and 55th minute.

The penalty king gave up his second opportunity of a hat-trick late on though as he gave Jermain Defoe the chance to make it 3-0, which the former England striker duly did.

A neat exchange on the counter attack a minute later saw Ryan Kent finish with a deft chip to round off a 4-0 win over a struggling St Mirren.

RANGERS: McGregor, Tavernier, Worrall, Katić, Barišić, Arfield, McCrorie (Jack 54), Davis (Candeias 64), Morelos, Defoe (Lafferty 83), Kent.
Subs not used: Foderingham, Halliday, Coulibaly, Middleton.

Wednesday 6th February 2019

Scottish Premiership
Aberdeen 2-4 Rangers
Goals: Morelos (2), Tavernier, Defoe

In this feisty encounter at Pittodrie, Alfredo Morelos opened the scoring as he expertly finished a rebound from a fierce Ryan Kent effort before Sam Cosgrove equalised for Aberdeen.

Then, a truly fantastic goal from Colombian striker Morelos. Kent drove at the Dons defence and slid a pass to Morelos who shaped a wonderful finish past Joe Lewis and low into the net with his left foot.

James Tavernier made it 3-1 from the spot as Aberdeen scored a spot kick of their own through Cosgrove, before Morelos and Scott McKenna were both given an early bath by the referee following an incident between the pair.

With the home side desperate for a leveller, the Gers broke on the counter and Tavernier picked out substitute Jermain Defoe, who emphatically finished into the back of the net to conclude the affair.

RANGERS: McGregor, Tavernier, Worrall, Goldson, Barišić, Arfield (Coulibaly 86), Jack, McCrorie, Candeias (Defoe 70), Morelos, Kent (Katić 83).
Subs not used: Foderingham, Halliday, Davis, Lafferty.

Wednesday 20th February 2019

Scottish Cup Fifth Round Replay
Rangers 5-0 Kilmarnock
Goals: Morelos (4), Halliday

It was Scottish Cup duty in this one as Rangers hammered Kilmarnock in the fifth round replay at Ibrox after a 0-0 stalemate at Rugby Park.

Alfredo Morelos loved scoring against Killie in 2018/19 as he notched another four on this February evening, with two in each half.

The first came before visiting goalie Daniel Bachmann was sent off, before a back post finish from the Colombian made it two going into half-time.

Andy Halliday swooped in to finish well for 3-0 before Morelos grabbed his hat-trick before a fourth, firstly thundering home before a low drive for his fourth, and Gers' fifth.

RANGERS: Foderingham, Tavernier, Goldson, Worrall, Barišić (Halliday 74), Jack, Candeias, Kamara (Lafferty 80), Arfield (Davis 73), Kent, Morelos.
Subs not used: Firth, Katić, Coulibaly, Defoe.

Sunday 24th February 2019

Scottish Premiership
Hamilton 0-5 Rangers
Goals: Jack, Defoe, Arfield, Tavernier, Lafferty

Steven Gerrard had watched his side put 13 goals past the opposition in the previous five games across league and cup competitions, and he was delighted to see another five go in here.

Rangers made it look so easy on the day as they hit Accies for five with some fantastic football; Ryan Jack curling in the first from 25 yards before Jermain Defoe's diving header from close range made it 2-0.

Scott Arfield then thumped in the third with a great strike before captain James Tavernier had a familiar feeling by striking home a penalty from 12 yards.

With the win wrapped up at half-time, the Gers naturally looked less of a threat in the econd period, but there was still room for 62nd minute substitute Kyle Lafferty to convert a low cross to make it 5-0.

RANGERS: McGregor, Tavernier, Goldson, Worrall, Halliday, Jack, Candeias, Kamara (Coulibaly 77), Arfield (Davis 62), Kent (Lafferty 62), Defoe.
Subs not used: Foderingham, Katić, Barišić, McCrorie.

Wednesday 27th February 2019

Scottish Premiership
Rangers 4-0 Dundee
Goals: Kamara, Tavernier, Morelos, Defoe

One of three new signings made in January, former Dundee midfielder Glen Kamara scored his first goal for Rangers against his former side in this game against Dundee.

The Finnish midfielder met a free-kick with a nice hit at the front post to get his side off to a great start before James Tavernier went from creator to scorer with a simple tap-in.

Alfredo Morelos made it 3-0 after just 23 minutes as he converted Canadian midfielder Scott Arfield's cut-back, with Jermain Defoe blasting in a fourth late on for a free-scoring Gers side.

RANGERS: McGregor, Tavernier, Goldson, Worrall, Barišić, Jack, Candeias (Defoe 66), Kamara, Arfield (Davis 45), Kent (McCrorie 73), Morelos.
Subs not used: Foderingham, Katić, Coulibaly, Lafferty.

Wednesday 3rd April 2019

Scottish Premiership
Rangers 3-0 Hearts
Goals: Defoe, Goldson, Arfield

After a narrow 2-1 defeat to Celtic effectively ended any hopes of a title in this campaign, Rangers knew they had to secure second place from Aberdeen and Kilmarnock, so there was plenty to play for as Hearts visited Glasgow.

Jermain Defoe gave his side an early lead as he struck the ball in off the underside of the crossbar after James Tavernier's shot was saved.

Tavernier then turned provider, as he so often did in this campaign, when he curled in a free-kick that was met by the head of Connor Goldson, the centre-back steering the ball home for 2-0.

Early in the second half the win was wrapped up as Tavernier's cross to Defoe saw the latter's shot saved by Zdenek Zlamal, but Arfield was on hand to finish it off.

RANGERS: McGregor, Tavernier, Goldson, Worrall, Flanagan, Davis, Jack (McCrorie 61), Arfield (Grezda 68), Kamara, Kent, Defoe (Lafferty 78).
Subs not used: Foderingham, Katić, Coulibaly, Candeias.

Sunday 7th April 2019

Scottish Premiership
Motherwell 0-3 Rangers
Goals: Arfield (3)

With Alfredo Morelos still suspended, Steven Gerrard persisted with a tweak to the formation that saw two narrow players place themselves close to Jermain Defoe and it worked a treat for a second game running.

Scott Arfield and Defoe linked up very well as the former claimed his first ever Rangers hat-trick at Fir Park. Firstly it was Defoe that prodded the ball through to Arfield, who converted his chance expertly.

The Gers then took advantage of lapse defending as Daniel Candeias fed Ryan Jack who in turn fed Arfield in the box, the midfielder striking the ball first time for a great finish.

Then, in the second half, Defoe showed a selfless streak as he beat a defender before slotting the ball over to the unmarked Arfield instead of going for goal himself, Arfield making no mistake to seal his hat-trick and the three points.

RANGERS: McGregor, Tavernier, Goldson, Katić, Flanagan, Jack, Kamara (Halliday 84), Candeias, Davis (Grezda 79), Arfield (McCrorie 71), Defoe.
Subs not used: Foderingham, Worrall, Lafferty, Middleton.

Saturday 20th April 2019

Scottish Premiership
Hearts 1-3 Rangers
Goals: Defoe, Jack, Katić

Rangers made it three wins in a row in this encounter at Tynecastle in the first of five post-split fixtures.

Glen Kamara's superb through ball cut open the Hearts defence but Jermain Defoe deserved plenty of credit for finishing the chance, as he steered the ball into the back of the net to give Gers the lead.

After 36 minutes it was 2-0. Ryan Jack won the ball from Oliver Bozanic and the midfielder followed up by taking full advantage of Daniel Candeias' through ball to score low into the far corner.

The Light Blues made it three shortly after the interval when Nikola Katić stretched at the back post from a short corner to convert in, while Hearts grabbed a consolation late on through Steven MacLean.

RANGERS: McGregor, Tavernier, Katić, Goldson, Flanagan, Jack, Davis (Polster 87), Kamara, Candeias (Middleton 72), Defoe (Lafferty 83), Arfield.
Subs not used: Foderingham, Worrall, Halliday, McCrorie.

Sunday 28th April 2019

Scottish Premiership
Rangers 2-0 Aberdeen
Goals: Tavernier (2)

The first of three home games to finish off the Ibrox fixtures for the season, the Gers got their first home win over the Dons in 2018/19 in comfortable fashion.

Penalties are James Tavernier's thing and he converted two in this league clash in the second half, the first coming after 48 minutes with Nikola Katić fouled.

The second came late on and made sure of the three points with the skipper scoring with ten minutes remaining on the clock, Gers all but making sure of a second place finish.

RANGERS: McGregor, Tavernier, Goldson, Katić, Flanagan, Jack, Kamara, Davis (McCrorie 84), Arfield, Kent (Candeias 84), Defoe (Wallace 87).
Subs not used: Foderingham, Worrall, Halliday, Middleton.

Sunday 5th May 2019

Scottish Premiership
Rangers 1-0 Hibernian
Goals: Defoe

Rangers sealed a fifth league win in a row for the first time in the campaign with a victory over Hibernian at Ibrox, in a typical end of season encounter.

Jermain Defoe did extremely well to finish in the first half in what turned out to be the only goal of the game.

Allan McGregor was given a red card late on after Steven Gerrard had made his three changes from the bench, so there was somewhat amusing few final minutes with midfielder Ross McCrorie handed the goalie top and gloves.

RANGERS: McGregor, Tavernier, Goldson, Katić, Flanagan, Jack, Davis, Kamara (McCrorie 80), Arfield, Defoe (Morelos 74), Kent (Candeias 45).
Subs not used: Foderingham, Worrall, Halliday, Barišić.

Sunday 12th May 2019

Scottish Premiership
Rangers 2-0 Celtic
Goals: Tavernier, Arfield

Rangers made it six victories on the spin in this final Old Firm derby as they produced a superb 90 minute display in front of a roaring Ibrox crowd.

The stadium was full to capacity as it had been for just about every home fixture in a long season across four competitions, and the fans were rewarded for their support with a second home derby win on the trot.

They got off to the perfect start after just two minutes when James Tavernier struck a free-kick with pace and power from the left, so much so that it evaded both sets of players in the box to find its way into the bottom corner.

Much like the first derby at Ibrox, the Gers had complete control over the match and had little trouble from Celtic all day. Indeed, the scoreline once more made it look a lot closer than how the match panned out in reality.

The Gers did make it a bigger winning margin than December's victory though, with Scott Arfield finishing off a great move. Glen Kamara's shimmy allowed him to drive with the ball away from Scott Brown before feeding Jermain Defoe, the striker cleverly dummying it to allow Arfield to run on to the ball and slide it low into the net.

RANGERS: Foderingham, Tavernier, Goldson, Katić, Flanagan, Davis (McCrorie 90), Jack, Kamara, Kent, Arfield (Candeias 83), Defoe (Morelos 79).
Subs not used: Firth, Barišić, Worrall, Halliday.

GUESS THE GER

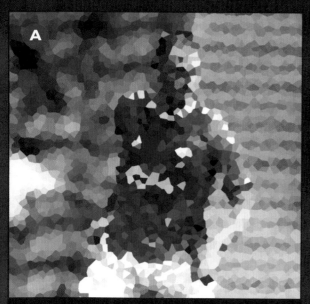

A

My first senior club was Neretvanac Opuzen before I signed for Slaven Belupo, both in my homeland. I signed for Rangers in 2018 and scored my first goal against Osijek.

B

I've played over 100 times for my country and won eight major trophies for Rangers. I scored my first Rangers goal against Werder Bremen in the UEFA Cup in 2008.

C

I play my football internationally for a country I was not born in, I have played for two Scottish clubs and two English clubs and I wear a special shirt number in memory of a friend.

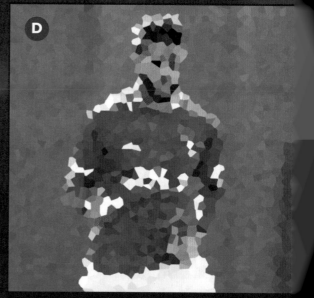

D

I was born in Wolverhampton but started my career at Shrewsbury Town. My middle name is Lambert and I scored against Hearts in the league twice last season.

ANSWERS ON PAGE 61

ARIBO AND OJO
JOIN THE GERS

Sheyi Ojo

Young winger Sheyi Ojo arrived from Liverpool on a season-long loan and joined his new Rangers teammates at the Hummel Training Centre for a week before flying out to the pre-season training camp in Portugal with the group. Upon signing on the dotted line at Ibrox, he outlined exactly why he chose Rangers to go on loan to...

"When I heard Rangers were interested I spoke to my representatives, the gaffer Steven Gerrard, and I spoke to Liverpool as well. I think all the parties believed this was the right destination for me, for my career and for this season.

"I spoke to Andy Firth and Ovie Ejaria and I know a few other players who play in this league as well. I think with all the advice I got it was an easy decision, there were other clubs I could have gone to, but I felt this was the right decision for me.

"It sounds stupid, but my other loans have taught me to just be myself, I think when I have gone on loan previously I have tried to fit in with the team. I have taken away from my own game but with this season and with the manager here backing me I am looking forward to being myself and playing how I naturally would. I think if I do that then it will be a very good season."

During the close season Rangers fans were eager to see their team return to action and naturally were itching to see new faces arrive at the club in the summer transfer window.

With the rumours picking up, it quickly emerged that Steven Gerrard wanted to add some creativity to his team from middle to front and by the end of June he signed two players precisely to that end.

Joe Aribo

Joe Aribo flew out to the Ibrox side's Algarve training camp as he was unveiled as a Gers player and he couldn't hide his delight. He said, "It is a dream come true to play for a club the size of Rangers. I grew up watching them, I am buzzing to be here and I can't wait to get going.

"I am quite dynamic and can get up and down the pitch. I can get at players in a 1v1 and sometimes I can pick a pass and find the back of the net. My aim last season was to get 10 goals and I achieved that. I want to be a goalscoring midfielder and I take pride and joy in scoring goals."

Aribo was full of praise for his now former club Charlton for showing faith in him and developing the midfielder and, after reminiscing about the Addicks' play-off final win at Wembley back in May, reckons the mentality there will stand him in good stead for the pressures of playing for a club the size of Rangers.

"They trusted me," Aribo said of his former team, "as I wasn't playing for an Academy at the age of 18, so they trusted me in bringing me in and developing me, and they really helped me a lot. It was surreal – there were so many fans and the atmosphere was bouncing. I couldn't hear my teammates next to me – it was just the best footballing moment I have had so far.

"We went out there expecting to win and we had to win, and that is what it is going to be like at a club the size of Rangers. You have to go out every week, perform and win games."

2018/19
EUROPA LEAGUE RUN

QUALIFIERS

Round One
July 2018

FK Shkupi
Home: 2-0 | Away: 0-0

Steven Gerrard managed his first competitive game in charge of Rangers with a 2-0 win over Shkupi from Macedonia at Ibrox. Jamie Murphy grabbed the opening goal midway through the first half to settle the nerves, but it wasn't until the 92nd minute that another goal came in the form of a James Tavernier penalty. With a decent lead to take over to the second leg, the Gers battled through the Skopje heat with a goalless draw, enough to see them progress on to the next round.

Round Two
July/August 2018

NK Osijek
Away: 0-1 | Home: 1-1

Just one week later, the first leg of the second round came around as the Light Blues travelled to Croatia to face tricky opposition in the form of Osijek. A well-worked corner and subsequent delivery from the right by Tavernier was followed by Alfredo Morelos' clever header, giving his side a vital early away goal. The Gers dug in to withstand the inevitable pressure from the home side and win the tie 1-0. An away goal was significant but with it just being one goal, it left the tie still on a knife edge for the Ibrox return leg. Nikola Katić's header against a side he used to play regularly against gave the Gers some breathing space, and despite a late equaliser by Borna Barišić the Gers progressed.

Round Three
August 2018

NK Maribor
Home: 3-1 | Away: 0-0

Next up on the European journey were Slovenian charges Maribor, who Scottish sides knew all about from previous European escapades, but Gerrard's side put in a magnificent display to win the first leg at Ibrox 3-1. Morelos grabbed a goal after six minutes before Gregor Bajde levelled before half-time. The Gers rallied though and got two late goals to ease any worries through a Tavernier penalty and Lassana Coulibaly. Playing a side that had recent Champions League experience, Rangers had to be intelligent in the Stadion Ljudski to ensure progression and they did that impressively. They earned a 0-0 draw, including a late penalty save from Allan McGregor, with a solid European away performance.

v FK Shkupi

Play-Off Round
August 2018

FC Ufa
Home: 1-0 | Away: 1-1

Rangers made it to the fourth set of qualifiers knowing they were 180 minutes away from the group stage, as they were drawn with relatively unknown Russian Premier League side Ufa. Another capacity crowd at Ibrox saw a nervy first-leg encounter, the Gers edging the match thanks to a solitary Connor Goldson effort. The second leg, a huge travelling distance away in central Russia, was even more nervy for the Rangers family. Ovie Ejaria scored a great curling effort early on, but Ufa equalised and later Jon Flanagan and Morelos were sent off. However, a monumental performance with nine men ensured a 1-1 draw on the night and qualification to the group stage – with all the glamour and financial rewards coming with it.

GROUP STAGE
Matchday One
20th September 2018

Villarreal
2-2

It was Rangers' first European group stage game since the 2010/11 Champions League campaign and the Gers fans travelled in large numbers yet again, this time to sunny Spain. Carlos Bacca scored from distance to give the Gers a rather cruel welcome back to the big stage, but as the game wore on the Gers came into it more and more. In the second half, Scott Arfield converted well from a Tavernier cross to level, though Gerard Moreno's almost instant response restored the La Liga side's advantage. Gerrard's men weren't done there though and continued to look for a way back into the game and got their rewards when a superb move down the left was finished off by Kyle Lafferty, giving the Gers a point in their first game.

v NK Osijek

Matchday Two
4th October 2018

Rapid Vienna
3-1 to Rangers

European nights under the floodlights at Ibrox are something else, and so it proved on this occasion with Rangers picking up the vital victory. Viton Berisha briefly stunned the home crowd before Morelos levelled with a typically predatory finish. The Gers were on top in the second half and their endeavours were rewarded in the 80th minute with a Tavernier spot kick before Morelos, assisted by a spectacular Daniel Candeias back heel, rolled in the third in injury time.

v Rapid Vienna

v Spartak Moscow

25th October 2018

Spartak Moscow
0-0

With four points on the board, a home tie with the Russians was a chance for Gerrard's charges to register another win and take charge of the group. Unfortunately, it didn't turn out that way as a frustrating 90 minutes followed. No one would have denied the Gers deserved a narrow win had they grabbed a goal, but it proved to be elusive as they failed to break down a stubborn Spartak rear guard.

8th November 2018

Spartak Moscow
4-3 to Spartak

The second trip of the group stage saw Rangers travel to the famous Russian capital of Moscow looking to take something from the match to make amends for the draw in the home fixture. What transpired was a goal-feast, with suspect defending on show from both sides, and unfortunately it was Spartak who took advantage more times. Roman Eremenko's own goal gave the Light Blues the lead before Lorenzo Melgarejo cancelled it out. Candeias' brilliant swivel and hit restored the Gers' lead, but Spartak came again as Goldson scored into his own net this time. Glenn Middleton grabbed his first European goal to send his side 3-2 ahead at the interval – but two quick-fire goals from Luiz Adriano and Sofiane Hanni in the second period gave Spartak the victory.

29th November 2018

Villarreal
0-0

Ibrox was packed to the rafters yet again for the final home game of the group with fans hoping for a victory to take into the final game in Austria. Despite a Candeias red card before half-time, the Gers put in a decent display against one of Spain's top teams from the season before but just couldn't carve that decisive opportunity to get the winner.

13th December 2018

Rapid Vienna
1-0 to Rapid Vienna

Despite the great start to the group stage, the results following meant that the Gers had to go to Vienna and win if they had any hope of qualifying through to the last 32 stage. The Light Blues just couldn't get going against the Austrian Bundesliga outfit and succumbed to a late winner from Dejan Ljubicic, sending the Gers out after a rather unexpected run in the competition in Gerrard's first few months of being in the Ibrox hotseat.

v Spartak Moscow

JAMES TAVERNIER

A TRIBUTE TO ERIC CALDOW

A defensive rock for Rangers and Scotland in the 1950s and 1960s, Eric Caldow sadly passed away at the age of 84 in March 2019.

Born in Cumnock in 1934, Caldow lived the dream of so many as he progressed through Rangers youth ranks and all the way into the first team at Ibrox. From 1953 until he departed for Stirling Albion in 1966, the full-back made over 400 appearances in the blue of Rangers.

Playing both right-back and left-back for club and country, Caldow missed just one game in 1958/59 as the Gers lifted the Scottish title,

and as captain he led his side out in the club's first ever European final in 1961, losing to Fiorentina in the Cup Winners' Cup.

Over his 13-year senior association with Rangers, Caldow won six league titles, five Scottish Cups and four League Cups, as well as being part of the Treble-winning squad of 1964. He also played in the club's European Cup semi-final appearance in 1960.

A member of the Scottish Football Hall of Fame since 2007, Caldow earned 40 caps for his country and played all three games of the 1958 World Cup. Caldow will go down as one of Rangers and Scotland's finest ever players to have worn the light and dark blue shirts.

RANGERS CROSSWORD

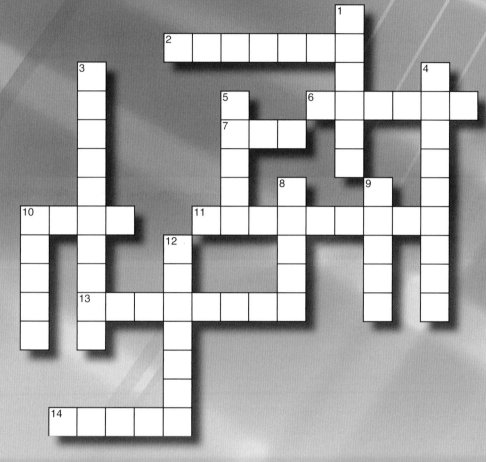

ACROSS

2   Where did Rangers spend a week training as part of pre-season preparations? (7)

6   Rangers won the Cup Winners' Cup in Spain but where was the opposition from? (6)

7   Rangers colours consist of blue, white and which other colour? (3)

10 A shortened version of the club's name. (4)

11 The club where Steven Gerrard made his name and became a legend. (9)

13 What English club did Rangers sign Joe Aribo from? (8)

14 Who did Rangers beat 4-2 on aggregate in the Battle of Britain in 1992/93? (5)

DOWN

1   A young Rangers forward from the Academy that made his senior debut in the last game of last season? (6)

3   Where did Rangers kick off their Scottish Premiership campaign? (10)

4   In which country did Rangers start their Europa league journey? (9)

5   Can you name Rangers' official club mascot? (5)

8   How many domestic trebles have the Gers won in their history? (5)

9   The area where Ibrox Stadium is located in Glasgow. (5)

10 Who famously lifted Rangers' ninth consecutive title aloft at Tannadice in 1997? (5)

12 Who was Rangers' top goalscorer last season with 30 goals? (7)

ANSWERS ON PAGE 61

JAMES TAVERNIER
GERS CAPTAIN

James Tavernier joined Rangers from Wigan Athletic in 2015, arriving at Ibrox in a £200,000 transfer as the Gers began their assault on the Scottish Championship. The Englishman soon became a fan favourite with his goals from free-kicks and general play impressing the crowds.

He continued that form over two seasons in the top flight after the club's promotion, but his fourth campaign gave supporters their best view of the attacking right-back as new boss Steven Gerrard appointed the Bradford-born star his club captain. Across the 2018/19 season, Tavernier scored a truly remarkable amount of goals alongside assists for his teammates. Being the club's first choice penalty taker does help with the goal aspect, of course, but you've still got to put them away and incredibly the skipper missed just one the

entire campaign, whilst also contributing goals from set-pieces and general play.

Tavernier leads by example on and off the field for the Ibrox side. He starts attacking moves from his side of the pitch more often than not, driving his side forward as they search for goals in domestic competitions as well as on the European stage home or away. His first goal of the 2018/19 season came in the Europa League first qualifying round, with Tavernier's late spot-kick

securing a 2-0 win over FK Shkupi in the first leg in Govan.

A 30th minute Tavernier kick from 12 yards gave his side, down to ten men, the lead in the first half of a tough opening Premiership clash away to Aberdeen and that was a familiar story throughout the campaign. Tavernier delivered time and time again from the penalty spot when it mattered, his goals helping the Gers reach the Europa League group stage and finish a comfortable lead of others in second place. He also grabbed his first Old Firm goal with a second minute free kick goal against Celtic in a 2-0 win in May. Tavernier hit the back of the net a total of 17 times across all competitions, beating his personal best from his debut season in the second tier and once again defeating John Greig and Sandy Jardine's scoring records for Gers defenders.

But not only does he chip in with a goal tally that many strikers would be proud of, he also assists his teammates with unbelievable consistency. Those 17 goals in 57 matches were complimented by 20 assists, a number some of the best midfielders and wingers sometimes fail to reach, never mind a defender. They came in the form of passes like his incisive forward ball to Ryan Kent as the winger scored at Celtic Park, or from brilliant crosses like his delivery for Alfredo Morelos' 88th minute winner at St Johnstone.

The marauding full-back is loving life in Glasgow, now into his fifth season as a Rangers player, and has shown just how invaluable he is to the club and for any success the Light Blues have.

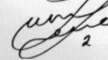

PLAYER OF THE YEAR

AWARDS

It was a season full of ups and downs for Rangers in 2018/19, playing in four competitions across the domestic and European scene. On the evening of April 7, it was all about the positives and focusing on the star performers for Steven Gerrard's side at the Player of the Year Awards, held at the Doubletree by Hilton hotel in Glasgow.

Colombian striker Alfredo Morelos was rewarded for his incredible goals tally of 30 in all competitions as he received three awards on the night. The first, named the Sam English Bowl, recognises the club's top scorer and Morelos won that comfortably. The next two would have given him a fantastic feeling as he scooped both Player of the Year, voted by fans, and Players' Player of the Year, decided by his teammates.

The fans also voted for Liverpool loanee Ryan Kent as the Young Player of the Year, a worthy reward for the young winger's performances over the campaign. Winner of the John Greig Achievement accolade was goalkeeper Allan McGregor, who enjoyed a stellar season on his return to Ibrox between the sticks. The final award was Goal of the Season, awarded to Ryan Jack for his Old Firm winner against Celtic at Ibrox halfway through the season.

ALFREDO MORELOS

" I think the support of my team is unconditional, their support has been fundamental for everything that I've achieved here with Rangers."

RYAN KENT

" A special mention has got to go out to all the fans and especially those who voted."

ALLAN MACGREGOR

" I call him [John Greig] 'ledge' because he is a legend and it means the world to me that he's picked me for this award."

RYAN JACK

" It means a lot. The goal on the day was a special moment for my family, for the fans and for my teammates and staff."

GERS
WORDSEARCH

```
W L L E M M U H F J T H W
P D N A L P O C M B R F R
J K W G L A S G O W N W M
Y A M O M M O L S F F A D
H H R R L S J G X Y G L E
C H W D R L I H O M A T U
T F T A I E O H R L G E L
I I E U R N G F B M O R B
P B T G R P E E I Z A N H
Z Q T L O T R Q Y J L N Y
B I M J E T S K K N S M K
K Y O X Z S D L E I F R A
K N Q J G E R R A R D N N
```

There are 20 Gers words hidden in the grid, but can you find them all?

Albertz	Follow	Hummel	Ojo
Arfield	Gerrard	Ibrox	Pitch
Bears	Glasgow	Jardine	Struth
Blue	Goals	Kit	Titles
Copland	Greig	Mols	Walter

ANSWERS ON PAGE 61

JORDAN
JONES

HISTORICAL A-Z OF RANGERS

AMERICA
Rangers have had several players from the United States on their books, from Claudio Reyna, DaMarcus Beasley and Maurice Edu to the present day with Matt Polster.

BARCELONA
The location of Rangers' European trophy success as Dynamo Moscow were defeated 3-2 at the Camp Nou in May, 1972.

COPLAND
The name of the 'east stand' at Ibrox, named after Copland Road which runs parallel to it. Known for years as 'the Rangers end'.

DE BOER
Rangers have been able to call on both De Boer brothers at Ibrox, with Ronald playing between 2000 and 2004 while Frank had a brief stint in 2003/04.

ENGLISH
The prolific Northern Irish striker Sam English, who played between 1931 and 1933 and holds the Rangers record for the most league goals scored in one season with 44 goals.

FIFTY-FOUR
The number of Scottish league titles Rangers have won to date, a world record.

GREIG
Voted the 'Greatest Ever Ranger' by supporters, John Greig spent his entire playing and managing career at the club, playing some 755 times while scoring 120 goals.

HUNDRED
Rangers' record league win percentage, one hundred per cent, during the 1898/99 season where they won all 18 games to lift the Scottish title.

IBROX
Rangers' home, a 51,000-seater stadium in Glasgow where supporters flock to cheer on the boys in blue every other Saturday.

JARDINE
A member of the 1972 European Cup Winners' Cup team, Sandy Jardine was a legend as a player and played a big part off the pitch for years afterwards before his passing.

KANCHELSKIS

The Russian winger Andrei Kanchelskis was a great servant to the club during his spell in Glasgow, spending four years at the Gers between 1998 and 2002.

LIVERPOOL

The club where manager Steven Gerrard made his name as a legendary midfielder, also the source of many Gers players in recent times such as Ryan Kent and Jon Flanagan.

McCOIST

The record goalscorer at Ibrox with 355 goals in a 15-year stint at the club, Ally McCoist also managed the Gers from 2011 to 2014.

NINE-IN-A-ROW

Rangers enjoyed magnificent success between 1988 and 1997 as the club won nine consecutive league titles in a row under Graeme Souness and then Walter Smith.

OLYMPIQUE LYONNAIS

The full name for the well-known French Ligue 1 club Lyon, where Rangers recorded a famous 3-0 away victory in the Stade de Gerland in the 2007/08 Champions League.

PETER

The first name of two of the founding fathers of the club – Peter McNeil and Peter Campbell. The other two were the former's brother Moses and William McBeath.

QUINTON

The left winger who played over 100 matches for the Light Blues between 1973 and 1976, Quinton Young.

RAMPANT

Rangers were rampant to say the least on Christmas Eve in 1898, defeating Hibernian 10-0 in the club's record league win.

SOUNESS

His arrival in 1986 as player-manager completely changed the Scottish football landscape for the Gers and Graeme Souness is still loved by fans to this day.

TRINIDAD & TOBAGO

Just two players who hailed from the small Caribbean islands can say they've played for Rangers: defender Marvin Andrews and midfielder Russell Latapy.

UGO

The English defender Ugo Ehiogu, who scored a memorable overhead kick for Rangers in a 1-0 win at Parkhead against Celtic in 2007. He tragically died in 2017.

VALLANCE

The first-ever club captain of the Gers, Tom Vallance skippered his side from 1876 to 1882.

WALTER

One of the club's most successful managers across two trophy-laden spells – the legendary Walter Smith.

XEREZ

One of two clubs Aaron Niguez was sent out on loan to from Valencia before he arrived at Rangers in 2008, Xerez CD are one of very few teams that have the letter X at the start of their name.

YOUNG

The first player to ever reach 50 caps for Scotland, George Young enjoyed 16 years at Rangers as a one-club man and won 12 major honours in that time.

ZURAB

The Georgian defender Zurab Khizanishvili, signed from Dundee who played 63 times over two seasons at Ibrox.

HELANDER IN BLUE

Arriving from Bologna in Italy, Filip Helander was one of several new additions to Steven Gerrard's squad in the summer. Huge centre-back Filip was very keen to experience the Ibrox atmosphere and run out on the famous pitch. Can you help the Swede find a way out of the big maze below so he can pull on that blue famous jersey?

ANSWER ON PAGE 61

WINNING
RESERVE LEAGUE

Rangers enjoyed a season of progress at first team level and that was continued by the Reserve team who brought silverware back to Ibrox.

The second-string side, led by head coach Graeme Murty, secured the SPFL Development League with a 3-1 victory over Falkirk in the last fixture, a fitting end to a superb campaign for the squad mostly made up of Under-20 and Under-18 players.

Of course, with it being Reserve football, several first team players were eligible to participate in games and many did throughout the 17 game season (Graham Dorrans, Gareth McAuley, Nikola Katic and Glen Kamara, to name a few). But it was the regular crop of youngsters playing consistently throughout the year that secured the success of being crowned champions.

The likes of Glenn Middleton – who balanced minutes for the Reserves with nearly 30 appearances for Steven Gerrard's first team – and Josh McPake were key to the title with plenty of goals and assists. Cameron Palmer (captain), Dapo Mebude and Stephen Kelly were mainstays of the team and all contributed massively over the season with consistent performances, doing their development as footballers the world of good.

Going into the final day away to Falkirk, it was set up to be a dead heat between Rangers and Celtic. Murty's Gers were level on points with their

GRAEME MURTY

rivals as well as Hibernian, with the latter having played all of their matches. In the end, Celtic's 3-2 win over St Johnstone ultimately didn't mean a thing as a 3-1 win for Gers secured the trophy on goal difference for the Light Blues.

RANGERS

TROPHIES

Scottish League Champions: 54

1891*, 1899, 1900, 1901, 1902, 1911, 1912, 1913, 1918, 1920, 1921, 1923, 1924, 1925, 1927, 1928, 1929, 1930, 1931, 1933, 1934, 1935, 1937, 1939, 1947, 1949, 1950, 1953, 1956, 1957, 1959, 1961, 1963, 1964, 1975, 1976, 1978, 1987, 1989, 1990, 1991, 1992, 1993, 1994, 1995, 1996, 1997, 1999, 2000, 2003, 2005, 2009, 2010, 2011

*The title in 1891 was shared with Dumbarton

Scottish Championship: 1
2016

Scottish League One: 1
2014

Scottish Third Division: 1
2013

Scottish Cup: 33

1894, 1897, 1898, 1903, 1928, 1930, 1932, 1934, 1935, 1936, 1948, 1949, 1950, 1953, 1960, 1962, 1963, 1964, 1966, 1973, 1976, 1978, 1979, 1981, 1992, 1993, 1996, 1999, 2000, 2002, 2003, 2008, 2009

Scottish League Cup: 27

1947, 1949, 1961, 1962, 1964, 1965, 1971, 1976, 1978, 1979, 1982, 1984, 1985, 1987, 1988, 1988–89, 1990–91, 1992–93, 1993–94, 1996–97, 1998–99, 2001–02, 2002–03, 2004–05, 2007–08, 2009–10, 2010-11

European Cup Winners' Cup: 1
1972 (Runners-up 1961, 1967)

UEFA Cup
Runners-up 2008

UEFA Super Cup
Runners-up 1972

RESULTS

Record Victory
13-0 vs Possilpark (Scottish Cup, October 1877), vs Uddingston (Scottish Cup, November 1877) and vs Kelvinside (Scottish Cup, September 1889)

Record League Cup Defeat
1-7 vs Celtic, League Cup Final, October 1957

Record League Win
10-0 vs Hibernian, December 1898

Record League Defeat
0-6 vs Dumbarton, May 1892

Most Goals in a Game
14-2 vs Blairgowrie, Scottish Cup, 1934 and vs Whitehill, Scottish Cup, 1883

Scottish League Cup Winners, 1992

Scottish Championship Winners, 2016

F.C. STATS

Sandy Archibald (L), Record League Appearances

OTHER:

Record Attendance
118,730 vs Celtic, Division One,
January 2nd 1939

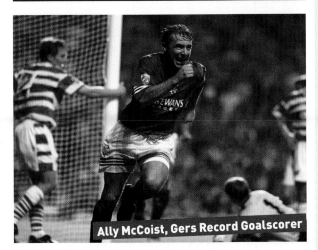
Ally McCoist, Gers Record Goalscorer

PLAYERS

Record Appearances
Dougie Gray, 948, 1925-27

Record League Appearances
Sandy Archibald, 513, 1917-34

Record Scottish Cup Appearances
Alec Smith, 74

Record League Cup Appearances
John Greig, 121

Record Euro Appearances
Barry Ferguson, 82

Record Goalscorer
Ally McCoist, 355 goals, 1983-98

Highest Goals in One Season
Jim Forrest, 57 goals, 1964-65

Highest League Goals in One Season
Sam English, 44 goals, 1931-32

Most League Goal
Ally McCoist, 251

Most Scottish Cup Goals
Jimmy Fleming, 44

Most League Cup Goals
Ally McCoist, 55

Most Euro Goals
Ally McCoist, 21

Most Capped Player
Ally McCoist, 61 caps for Scotland

ALKASS

INTERNATIONAL CUP

Back in February of 2019, Rangers made their debut in the prestigious Alkass International Cup, a youth competition in Qatar, and it couldn't have gone any better for the young Gers.

In the group stage, Rangers began their journey with a 3-0 victory over Raja Casablanca. Cole McKinnon and Kai Kennedy grabbed the goals to see the young Gers comfortably leading at the interval, with an injury time second half goal from Matty Yates clinching the opening win over their Moroccan opposition.

Local side Aspire Academy were up next, inflicting the Gers' first defeat in a 3-1 win with Yates grabbing the solitary Gers goal. To the quarter final, and in their way were Tunisian outfit Étoile Sahel, who were swept away in a huge victory for the Light Blues. Nathan Young-Coombes and Chris McKee both scored hat-tricks and Aaron Lyall also got on the scoresheet in a thumping 7-0 win.

The conquerors of Real Madrid in the form of Japanese youngsters Kashiwa Reysol were the opposition in the semi-final, but another superb 90 minutes from Rangers ensured a 5-1 win. Kennedy grabbed a double with Young-Coombes and Lyall once again scoring and substitute Alex Lowry completing the scorers.

To the final and Italian outfit Roma, who opened the scoring before a red card for each team all in the first half. Ciaran Dickson levelled and the game finished 1-1, with a penalty shoot-out required. An epic set of kicks was followed by Kennedy (named player of the tournament) scoring the decisive penalty, with the Gers winning 9-8 and lifting the trophy.

SCOTTISH YOUTH CUP
WIN

Season 2018/19 went down as a fantastic campaign of success for the Rangers youngsters in the Under-18 category. With the Alkass Cup secured, the Gers youngsters added the Club Academy Scotland league and the SFA Youth Cup to their trophy haul.

Players like Kyle McClelland, Ciaran Dickson, Ben Williamson, Kai Kennedy and Nathan Young-Coombes were fantastic all season for David McCallum's side in a trophy-laden campaign, with many of that crop being utilised from time-to-time in the older Reserve group by Graeme Murty.

After the Alkass Cup success in February, the Gers added a second cup at the end of April as they defeated Celtic at Hampden to lift the Youth Cup. The Ibrox side were two up after six minutes following strikes by midfielder Dickson and forward Dapo Mebude, before Celtic grabbed two goals of their own at the start of the second half. But the Gers rallied and Young-Coombes' thumping header won it for the Light Blues.

Clinching the league title against Hearts with a 3-1 win a week later, the Gers ensured qualification for the first time to the UEFA Youth League for the 2019/20 season, meaning this exciting crop of young talent will be competing against Europe's best in a competitive tournament, adding to their already impressive development.

RANGERS W.F.C.

Women's football is a game on the rise in Scotland, throughout the world, and Rangers as a club have long embraced the sport.

In 2008 Rangers sealed a partnership with Paisley City Ladies to form Rangers Ladies. The team played in the third tier of Scottish Women's football in their first year and were crowned league winners at the first time of asking. After lifting the Scottish Women's First Division trophy, Rangers have grown from strength to strength.

The decision was taken in 2018 to rename the club from Rangers Ladies to Rangers Women. The Blue Belles are now an established Scottish Women's Premier League club and after playing at various venues over the last few years – including New Tinto Park in Glasgow – the Gers are now back at the training ground sharing the facilities with the first team squad and Academy teams at the Hummel Training Centre.

In July, Rangers revealed that the women's first-team and academy became fully integrated with the club's football department. The board committed to increased investment in November 2018 and the changes were made in the summer of 2019, allowing the club to recruit professional players and convert some existing players into professionals as well.

Amy McDonald, who moved from head coach to Women's and Girls' football manager at the time of the announcement, expressed her delight at the positive move by the club; "This is a truly significant move for Rangers and women's football within Scotland. As one of the leading clubs in the UK on the men's side of the game, this commitment now means we can start to bring the Women's and Girls' programme in line with that.

"The Academy has seen tremendous success of late after similar investment in recent years and I am excited by the potential we now have here. This gives us the opportunity to recruit better players who are established within the game, which in turn helps Rangers improve performances and results on the pitch."

Under McDonald, Rangers came fourth in the Premier League in the 2018 season and played the first half of the 2019 campaign under her stewardship. Gregory Vignal arrived for the second half, finishing in mid-November.

The Frenchman has a few special players to work with in the squad and one of those is midfielder Jade Gallon. At the summer break in the season, she was Rangers' top league scorer with four and was nominated for the SWPL Player of the Month award in April, as she grabbed vital goals at Motherwell and Spartans. The No. 10 continues to be a danger to any opposition.

Attacker Carla Boyce, who arrived from champions Glasgow City in February 2018, provides the side with a goal threat in the forward areas. An up-and-coming star is the young forward Laura McCartney, the only Rangers player named in the Scotland squad for the Under-19s European Championships that took place over the summer.

With the fantastic all-round success of the FIFA Women's World Cup back in June and July, it's hoped that the profile of the women's game and therefore the fan numbers will increase. Scotland of course qualified and were unlucky to not make it out of their group. Their squad included Erin Cuthbert, a former Rangers player with a great story.

Let's hope the Rangers Women can continue to attract more supporters to cheer them on in their endeavours for success and development in the women's game.

As one of the leading clubs in the UK on the men's side of the game, this commitment now means we can start to bring the women's and girls' programme in line with that.

Amy Macdonald

RANGERS CHARITY FOUNDATION
A FORCE FOR GOOD!

You've seen Rangers play well on the pitch, but did you know that they can be a force for good off it as well?

The Rangers Charity Foundation shows compassion to those in need, helps to tackle inequalities and creates opportunities for people of all ages to change their lives for the better.

Each season, the Foundation delivers projects to thousands of people across a range of areas including employability, education, health and wellbeing, as well as diversity and inclusion. From getting fit and learning about healthy eating, to visually impaired football and gaining qualifications – there's something for everyone!

The Foundation is also passionate about making dreams come true for fans going through a tough time. People impacted by disability, illness or other difficulties can enjoy special experiences with the Rangers first team and manager to help create a day they'll never forget.

Other local, national, international and Armed Forces charities are also supported with donations each season.

And you can get involved with the Rangers Family too! The Foundations hosts fundraising activities for all ages and abilities each year. Fancy running around the Ibrox pitch covered in blue paint? The Blue All Over Fun Run is just one of a fun calendar of events ready for you to enjoy.

To see how you can get involved visit the website at
www.rangerscharity.org.uk or find them on social media!

BIG GERS QUIZ

True or False: Steven Gerrard made James Tavernier captain at the start of the 2018/19 season.

Jermain Defoe arrived from which English Premier League club on loan last January?

Which age group did Gerrard coach at Liverpool before he made the move to Ibrox?

Who scored Rangers' first competitive goal this season?

And who was the opposition?

In what year were Rangers formed?

How many points did the Gers finish on last season?

And how many goals did the team score?

Which international team does Glen Kamara represent?

And who else on the club's books can play for that nation?

11. Which two former strikers were named in the Greatest XI by fans?

12. In which city did Rangers lift their only European trophy to date?

13. What is the club's most famous song sung by the supporters?

14. What nationality is summer signing Filip Helander?

15. True or False: Greg Docherty's loan spell last season in England was for Bury in League 2.

16. What significant moment in the history of Rangers happened in 1997?

17. How many league titles have Rangers won?

18. What song – and by whom was it sung – is played when the teams enter the Ibrox pitch?

19. Who captained Rangers to their last domestic treble to date?

20. Who is the current Rangers No.2?

RANGERS
SOCCER SCHOOLS

BE SIMPLY THE BEST

RANGE OF COURSES AVAILABLE FOR ALL AGES AND ABILITIES

For more information call **0141 580 8819**
email **soccerschools@rangers.co.uk** or visit **rangers.co.uk**

ANSWERS

Guess the Ger P31

Player 1: Nikola Katić

Player 2: Steven Davis

Player 3: Scott Arfield

Player 4: Connor Goldson

Crossword P41

Wordsearch P46

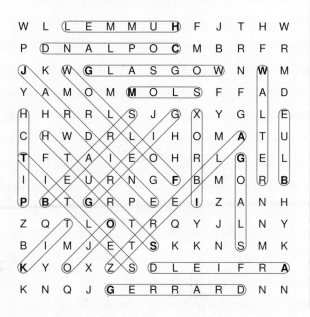

Maze P50

Big Gers Quiz P59

1. True
2. AFC Bournemouth
3. Under-18
4. Ryan Jack
5. St Joseph's
6. 1872
7. 78 points
8. 82 goals
9. Finland
10. Serge Atakayi
11. Ally McCoist and Mark Hateley
12. Barcelona
13. Follow Follow
14. Swedish
15. False – Greg Docherty's loan spell was for Shrewsbury Town in League 1
16. The Gers won nine league titles in a row.
17. 54 titles
18. Simply the Best by Tina Turner
19. Barry Ferguson
20. Gary McAllister

61

WHERE'S BROXI?